Basic Life Principles 1

Basic Life Principles 1

A Book for Raising Virtuous children

Chinonye Oluoha

3

PUBLISHER

Cover design by

ISBN Trade Paper:
ISBN EBook:

For Worldwide Distribution, Printed in the Nigeria.

1 2 3 4 5 6 / 19 18 17 16

Dedication

To all the children of the world.

Contents

Introduction

Dear children,

Here is a book teaching you virtues. Virtues means things you need to know and do in order to have good character and become great in the future.

In this book you'll find wonderful lessons, pictures and stories about how good behavior can help people stay out of trouble and also help them to become successful in life.

I hope this book will help you a lot to develop good character and then to become the great person that you should be in the future because the world needs a lot more of great people like you.

Chinonye Oluoha

How to Use Basic Life Principles

(For Families)

Parents should pick out a suitable day and time. At that time, every member of the family should gather at the sitting room, study room or praying room with a copy of BLP (Basic Life Principles) for each person including daddy and mummy. Everyone sits down uprightly and comfortably and then the daddy, mummy or any appointed person takes a lead. It is advisable to begin with a prayer of thanksgiving and commitment. After which the leader should choose a topic (It could be better organized to go from lesson one to lesson twenty. Though, this is up to the family to decide).

The topic should be announced and pronounced accurately. The meaning of the topic should be read out and everyone should be giving a chance to give their own meaning to the word. It is encouraged that the leader reads out the bible text directly from the bible. And everyone should get a chance to share their thought about the topic. For example, the leader could ask: what do you think about forgiveness? This could be thought revealing.

Thereafter, the leader reads out or appoints someone to read out clearly and loudly the lesson and the story.

The quote: To be read out and explained by the leader.

Things to do: This is a kind of assignment. Parents must ensure that the children carry out this assignment. It is the practical aspect of the lesson and should be taken seriously.

What did you learn: This serves as a test but there shouldn't be a right or wrong answer as long as is in line with morals and virtues. Those who can write should put down what they have learnt and take turn to read out what they have written.

Questions: This should be interactive and should never cause tension. Parents should correct their wrongs and encourage them to pay more attention next time.

Lesson One

Patience /peɪʃns/

Meaning: To wait and endure nicely without complaining and murmuring.

Bible Text: Through patience a ruler can be persuaded—Proverbs Chapter 25:15.

Thought: Can't I get the things I want a little quicker?

Yes! You may not get the things you want as quickly as you want them and this is because there is time for everything: snacks time, food time, bed time, play time, TV time, study time and so on. When you do things outside their time, it brings confusion and problems. But if you want to live a great life, then you must learn to be patient. When you want something and cannot get it immediately then you must be willing to wait because patience is a fruit of the Holy Spirit—a virtue and a quality for living a great life.

It is necessary for growth and maturity. It helps us to be able to start and complete a task. This means that when you are patient you'll be able to start something and to complete it without giving up half way. Patience helps people to become successful and to get exactly the things they desire. It brings orderliness. It helps to develop better relationship with people and it helps us to have peace and joy. It takes patience to learn, to grow, to develop and to become great in life.

When people are patient they can wait for their turn without grumbling. They will obey traffic lights and laws. They will be calm in stressful situations and will not commit any crime for success.

Even though patience can be difficult, it is still very rewarding. Therefore, you need to be patient with God, with your parents, with your siblings, with your teachers and with everyone and must learn to wait for the right times for the things you want.

When you pray – wait for your answers.
When you make a request – wait for your demand.

When you plant – wait for it to grow.
When you work – wait for your reward.

Truly, good things come to those who wait.

Story: The Reward of Patience

A daddy told his two children, "Be patient, when I receive my salary, I will buy both of you some fine toys." The younger son was impatient; he worried until his daddy was forced to buy him what he was able to afford—an ugly old toy. The older son waited until his daddy received his salary and bought for him a beautiful big toy. And this is how rewarding patience can be.

Quote: "Good things come to those who wait."

Things to do: Pour some sand in an empty tin or glass and plant a bean in it. Water it daily and wait for it to grow.

Questions:

1. What should you do when you cannot get the things you want as soon as you want them?
2. Why should you wait if you cannot get your desires at the time you want them?
3. Even though patience is difficult, it is still very what?
4. What are the rewards of patience?
5. Good things come to those who do what?

WHAT DID YOU LEARN FROM THIS LESSON?

LESSON TWO

SHARING /ʃerɪŋ/

Meaning: Sharing is to give someone a portion of what belongs to you.

Bible text: One man gives freely yet gains even more; another withholds unduly but comes to poverty - Proverbs Chapter 11:24.

Thought: Why do I have to share what belongs to me?

Nobody in this life has everything they want. There is something that someone has that others don't have. You are more privileged, blessed, favored and intelligent than somebody. Your parents can provide for you more than some parents can provide for their children.

You must therefore, learn to share the things you have got with others who don't have as much as you have. If you spend more time worrying about what is yours, you will lose out but when you share, you gain more. You gain happiness, friendship, love, and togetherness.

If feels good to give and it is fun to share. You can share your food, snacks, clothes, juice, candy, toy, games, books, crayons and pencils. You can also share your smiles, laughter and then your time and friendship.

And when you reach out to others, others will in turn reach out to you. There is indeed, love in sharing.

Story: Dino Learnt How to Share

There was a boy called Dino, he lived in a neighborhood where there were lots of children. His parents bought him lots of toys to play with but Dino was very stingy, he hates to share. Some of his neighbors often came around to play with him but Dino's words were always, "Go away! Don't play with my toys." Dino eventually scared all the other kids away and they left him alone.

A day came when Dino got tired of playing all by himself. He became very lonely, sad and bored that he started to need a friend seriously. From his window, he watched the other children happily share and play together and he admired them so deeply.

One day, he got an idea. He packed up some of his toys, went to meet the other children and politely said to them, "I brought some toys, can we share?" They welcomed him, shared their toys together and their play was a lot more fun. From then, Dino made friends and became a happy boy.

Quote: "There is love in sharing."

Things to do: Practice sharing everything you get with someone for a week.

Questions:

1. What are the things you can gain from sharing?
2. Why should you share with others?
3. Who should you share with?
4. What are the things you have that you can share with others?
5. There is love in what?

WHAT DID YOU LEARN FROM THIS LESSON?

LESSON THREE

LOVE /lʌv/

Meaning: Showing an unconditional kindness to people.

Bible text: Beloved, let us love one another for love is of God and anyone who loves is born of God and knows God – 1 John Chapter 4:7.

Thought: Do I have to love the people whom I don't feel good about?

How you feel about people should not determine how you should treat them. God first loved us even when we did not deserve his love and so you should be kind and good to everyone no matter how you feel about them.

Love is the most important thing in life; it brings happiness, joy and peace. Everyone needs love and when you give love to people, you have given them the most important thing in life.
You can love by showing kindness, by sharing, by forgiving, by tolerating, by treating people nicely, by respecting, by caring, by giving a helping hand, by praying for others and by being friendly.

You should treat people nicely regardless of how they treat you because love is a sacrifice.

Story: Donald and the Love Cake

Once upon a time, there was a boy named Donald who went to a school where there was no love. His schoolmates hated one another, bullied and fought with each other. Donald hated to go to school each morning and this troubled his parents.

One day, Donald came back from school and complained to his mom how people had quarreled and fought in his school and his mom sat him down and spoke to him. She said to him "Donald my son, the reason why there is no peace and happiness in your school is because there is no love. But I'm going to bake for you a love cake which will bring love to your school and you only need to believe that sharing the cake to everyone will make them love one another." She also told him that she would bake the cake with tolerance, giving, sharing, patience, respect, kindness and politeness.

The next day, Donald took the love cake to school and every one became surprised to see a love cake in a school where there was no love. He called his school mates together and told them that what they needed to bring peace and happiness in their school was love and after speaking to them, he shared the cake amongst them. Even though everyone got just a piece, the cake brought love into their hearts and they all loved one another. And because of this love, peace and happiness also dwelt in their school and they all enjoyed their school. From then, Donald was appreciated and recommended and this made him very happy.

Quote: "Love makes the world a better place."

Things to do: Think out and do something for someone that will show love.

Questions:

1. Should you love the people that you don't feel good about?
2. How should you treat the people who don't treat you well?
3. What is the most important thing in life?
4. How can you show love?
5. How does love make the world a better place?

WHAT DID YOU LEARN FROM THIS LESSON?

LESSON FOUR

Smile /smaɪl/

Meaning: A smile is to happily open the front part of your teeth to show that you are happy, kind, pleased or grateful.

Bible Text: If I say, I will forget my complaint, I will put off my sad face and wear a smile – Job Chapter 9:27.

Thought: Won't my cheek hurt if I wore a smile all the time?

A smile can't hurt your cheek; it rather beautifies your face. A frown can wrinkle your face and make you look ugly and old. It also makes you look unhappy and looking unhappy can scare people away from you.

You should always put on a smile because it will make you look happy even if you are not. It makes you look pretty, younger and attractive. It can make you feel good and can also make others feel good and happy.

It helps you to be relaxed and to stay healthy. It can also help you to make friends easily and then can bring good luck to you.

Story: Ona and Her Good Luck

There was a girl named Ona who had good luck all the time. She was always happy and would always wear a beautiful smile. And her friends wondered why she had good things happen to her all the time. They became jealous of her and were unhappy because they wished that good things could also happen to them so that they would be as happy as their friend Ona.

Yemisi, one of Ona's friends decided that she was going to spy on Ona to find out the source of her good luck. So one day, she discovered that Ona's secret of good luck was her smile and she decided to try out the secret.

She started smiling to everyone she met even when she was not happy and she observed that people became friendly to her and this also brought her a lot of good luck. From then henceforth, she wore the biggest smile and got the biggest good luck.

Quote: "A smile is the prettiest thing you can wear."

Things to do: Give everyone you meet a beautiful smile.

Questions:

1. What do smiles do to your face?
2. What are the things that a smile can do for you?
3. What can a frown do for you?
4. What is the prettiest thing you can wear?
5. When was the last time you smiled?

WHAT DID YOU LEARN FROM THIS LESSON?

LESSON FIVE

Giving /gɪvɪŋ/

Meaning: To let somebody have something that belongs to you.

Bible Text: Give and it will be given to you: Good measure, pressed down, shaken together and running over – Luke Chapter 6:38.

Thought: Won't people have more than me when I give them what I have?

If you want to be blessed then you must learn how to give. It often seems like you lose when you give but what actually happens is that you give yourself an opportunity to receive. Giving gives you a lasting happiness. It causes you to receive and to be blessed.

There are lots of things you can give: A smile, an advice, an encouragement, your time, treasure and talent, a helping hand, food, toys, clothes and even friendship.

You should give to those in need, to the sick, to the poor and to everyone that needs your help. When you give, you help people and you also make them happy. Giving is an act of love and so when you give, you show love.

Story: How Joel Received His Wish

Joel became an unhappy kid because he had not gotten the bicycle that he had desperately wished for. His parents had often told him that they could not afford the bicycle at the time and this had always annoyed him.

On one give-away day, Joel decided to give away all his games which he had long stopped playing with. He went to some kids in his neighborhood and gave them all his games. He observed that the kids were all excited and happy and this cheered him up.

As soon as he got back home, he saw a beautiful red bicycle packed by his house. He rushed inside the house and his mother informed him that one of their neighbors had brought the bicycle as a give-away gift to Joel because he had got more than one. Joel was very surprised and happy. He had also learnt that when you give, you will also receive.

Quote: "The person who gives with a smile is the best giver because God loves a cheerful giver."- Mother Theresa.

Things to do: Find out what you can give to about 5 people that will make them happy.

Questions:

1. What must you do in order to be blessed?
2. What happens when you give?
3. What are some of the things you can give?
4. When you give, do you lose?
5. What do you show when you give?

WHAT DID YOU LEARN FROM THIS LESSON?

LESSON SIX

Politeness /pəlaɪtnəs/

Meaning: To have good manners and good behavior.

Bible text: To speak evil of no one, to be peaceful, gentle, showing all humility to all men –Titus Chapter 3:2.

Thought: Won't people think I'm too easy, stupid, boring and pretending?

Good manners and good behavior is very important for people to live together peacefully. To be able to live peacefully with each other is something that we must all learn to do and one of the things that you have to do in life is to let people learn good manners from you.

When you are polite, you respect others, greet them, ask for their permission, apologize when you hurt them and speak to them in a friendly and gentle manner.

Rudeness and disrespect causes a lot of trouble and fights amongst people but when you choose to be polite, you will be peaceful and will also be a good example to others. People will feel good about helping you, will love and appreciate you and you'll also make friends easily.

Story: The Troublesome Boy

There was a boy that caused trouble and fought with people all the time and so everyone called him the troublesome boy. He didn't say: Please, I'm sorry, may I, excuse me, you're welcome, thank you, and forgive me. And he was rude and disrespectful.

One day as he was alone and tired of being alone because he had no friends, a gentleman walked up to him and asked him why he wasn't playing with his friends. He angrily and rudely told the man that he didn't have any friend because nobody liked him. And quickly the man observed how rude he was and gently taught him how to be polite. He told him to always start his interaction with please and to end it with thank you. And he also taught him to always use the polite words.

The troublesome boy decided that he was going to start using these words and everywhere he went, people observed that he had become polite and that made him to have friends. He taught his friends to always use these words and from then, he was no longer known as the troublesome boy.

Quote: "Good manners can bring you good success."

Things to do: Make courtesies and politeness a habit by practicing them every day.

Questions:

1. What are the good things that being polite can cause?
2. Mention five polite words?
3. What should you always use in order to avoid trouble?
4. Do you think anybody likes to be shown rudeness or disrespect?
5. What will good manners and good behavior do for you?

WHAT DID YOU LEARN FROM THIS LESSON?

LESSON SEVEN

Revenge /rɪvendʒ/

Meaning: Treating people badly in order to give them what they deserve.

Bible text: Shouldn't you have had mercy on your fellow servant just as I had on you? – Matthew Chapter 18:33.

Thought: If I don't revenge, how will my offenders learn their lessons?

There are many ways you can teach your offenders a positive lesson: you can show love, mercy, forgiveness, kindness, tolerance, patience and so on.

Revenge causes you to be offensive just like the offender and can only cause more troubles and regrets. When someone hurts you, don't act quickly. Take a few moments to calm your tension. Practice breathing in and out for some time or you can leave the place or scene.

You must never take the law into your own hands otherwise you will be equally guilty. You have to let your parents, teachers or the police know about the people who hurt or trouble you.

You also have to know that justice belongs to God and must learn to let God carry out His job. In life, people hurt people. People will hurt you and you will hurt other people. This is why you must decide to forgive, love, tolerate or report but never to revenge.

Story: Angela and Kate were two sisters who always fought over everything: Toys, games, candies, snacks, clothes, shoes, TV programmes and so on.

One day, while Angela was eating some chocolate, she mistakenly stained Kate's doll. Kate was deeply offended and even though Angela had apologized to her, she still didn't forgive and wanted to revenge. She brought out one of Angela's finest dresses and was about to cut it into pieces when she accidentally cut off half of one of her fingers.

Her short finger had continued to remind her of the danger of revenging and she had never stopped to regret.

Quote: "An eye for an eye makes the whole world blind." – Mahatma Gandhi

Things to do: Practice forgiving your offenders instead of revenging and experience how peaceful you can be.

Questions:

1. What are the ways you can teach your offenders positive lessons?
2. When you revenge, are you also as guilty as your offender?
3. Who is the right person to carry out justice, you or God?
4. What are the bad things that revenge can cause?
5. An eye for an eye makes the whole world —————?

WHAT DID YOU LEARN FROM THIS LESSON?

LESSON EIGHT

Hygiene /haɪdʒin/

Meaning: Taking care of your body in order to stay healthy and strong.

Bible text: Beloved I pray that you may prosper in all things and be in health just as your soul prospers – 3 John verse 2.

Thought: This can be a lot of work.

Taking care of yourself is the most important work that you have to do. If you do not take care of your body, you'll certainly fall sick. This is because dirtiness attracts germs and bacteria which cause infections and diseases.

To avoid germs, you must try to always be clean: Brush your teeth and take your bathe twice a day, in the morning and in the night. Wash your hands regularly especially after playing or using the toilet. Don't put dirty things in your mouth. Keep your nails short and clean, don't pick your nose with your fingers instead use tissue paper or handkerchief.

Wash your fruits and vegetables before eating them, wear clean clothes and shoes, wash your hair thoroughly and so on. And when you protect yourself, you'll not get infected.

To stay healthy, you must also sleep well; early to bed, early to rise makes someone healthy, wealthy and wise. Eat foods that have carbohydrate, proteins and vitamins and never forget to drink a lot of water.

Story: Mr. Bacteria found a Home

Mr. Bacteria travelled to every place in search of dirty people to infect. He entered a school one day and was happy to have finally found a place to live because almost all the children in that school were dirty.

They played a lot with sand and dirt and used the toilets without washing their hands afterwards. They didn't brush their teeth or take their bathe properly and regularly. They wore dirty uniforms and also littered their school and environment with waste. All this caused them to look dirty and also to smell so badly.

Mr. Bacteria then infected them and almost all of them fell sick and were always sick. But there was a boy whose name was John who Mr. Bacteria could not infect because he was very hygienic. When everyone in the school noticed that John didn't fall sick, they quickly understood that it was because he was hygienic and did all that will make him stay healthy.

This made them to also start practicing hygiene and this became a big trouble for Mr. Bacteria because he didn't have anywhere to live again and so he packed his bags and left their school forever.

Quote: "Cleanliness is next to Godliness."

Things to do: Experience how wonderful you'll look and feel when you practice hygiene and cleanliness.

Questions

1. What is the most important work for you to do?
2. What are some of the things you have to do in order to avoid Mr. Bacteria?
3. What are the things that can attract Mr. Bacteria?
4. What are the things that dirtiness can cause?
5. Cleanliness is next to what?

WHAT DID YOU LEARN FROM THIS LESSON?

LESSON NINE

Courage /kɜrɪdʒ/

Meaning: To be bold and fearless.

Bible text: Be strong and of good courage; do not be afraid for the Lord your God is with you wherever you go—Joshua Chapter 1:9.

Thought: Will I be able to conquer my fears?

Fear is like fire. It can grow out of control when you feed it with your imagination. If you give fear a chance, it will grip you and control your life. But if you defeat it, you'll be amazed at how much happy, great and healthy you can be.

God wants you to be courageous because to be courageous is to know that He is with you always and will save you from bad things. A courageous person can boldly speak out, face and overcome difficult times and become a world champion. There would be tough times in life but with courage, you'll always overcome. To overcome fear, you must not let your mind to think negative, evil or bad things. When you practice this, you will notice that you actually have nothing to fear about.

Fear gives birth to shyness and doubt and when you defeat fear, you would have defeated its children. Nobody enjoys being with timid, fearful and shy people and so you have to be courageous, bold and fearless. You have to boldly tell people what you think and feel but in a very polite way.

To be courageous does not include playing with fire, sharp or dangerous objects. It simply means to do the right things boldly.

Story: The Fearful Diana

Diana lived in a big house with her parents. She had a room to herself, a playground and plenty of dolls to play with. But Diana could not enjoy all of this comfort that her parents provided her with because she was always afraid. She feared the dark, shadows, thunders and sometimes she even feared her own dolls. Diana also did not have any friends because she was too shy and timid and so nobody enjoyed playing with her. Her parents were very displeased with all these and wanted her to overcome shyness and fear in order to be a happy kid and then, they took her to her Aunt's house that had two courageous boys.

Oftentimes, Diana's cousins would frighten her because they enjoyed how she feared too many things. Her constant screams and wails disturbed her Aunt who persuaded her too many times not to fear things but Diana was still always afraid.

One day, her Aunt got an idea and took her to a psychologist who advised Diana that to be bold and courageous that she must start using her imagination rightly. She told her to stop imagining the wrong things and to start imaging herself to be a great child who can freely interact with others and express herself. And that she should always imagine God and His Angels watching over her and keeping her safe.

After that day, Diana started using her imagination rightly and then she discovered that she was no longer afraid of too many things. When she finally got back home, her parents were very happy to know that their daughter had become bold and courageous.

Quote: "It takes courage to do the right things and achieve great things."

Things to do: Try to always imagine only good and positive things because this is a sure way to conquer fear.

Question:

1. What makes fear to grow?
2. Why does God want you to be courageous?
3. What are the benefits of being courageous?
4. What are the things that being courageous does not include?
5. What are you supposed to use rightly in order to become courageous?

WHAT DID YOU LEARN FROM THIS LESSON?

LESSON TEN

Prayer /preə(r)/

Meaning: Talking to God in word or in thought.

Bible Text: Pray without ceasing—1 Thessalonians Chapter 5:17.

Thought: Does God listen when I pray?

God loves to hear you talk to Him because He is your father and you are His child. He cares about you and promises to always love you. When you pray, you connect yourself with God, your heavenly father. You tell Him your needs, your wish and all that is happening in your life.

Even though God knows you personally but He still enjoys hearing you speak to Him about your life and about everything that concerns you. You can tell God everything that you want Him to do for you. God may sometimes not say yes to all your wishes and requests but when He says No, it is simply because He knows exactly what is best for you and desires to give you only what is best for you.

When you pray, you should praise and worship God and ask Him to show you mercy. Tell Him about yourself, Parents, siblings, friends, those you love and also about everyone who need your prayers because God does not want to only bless you but to also bless everyone that you care about.

Story: The Missing Car Key

Peter played with his daddy's car key and eventually, he lost it. He searched everywhere for it but didn't find it. He became very angry and scared because he knew that his daddy would scold and spank him when he finds out about his missing car key. He started crying and cried until his eyes were swollen but he did not remember to pray. He sat down and wondered what next to do then he suddenly remembered to pray.

Then he prayed, "Dear God, I'm sorry for being careless with my daddy's car key but please, help me to find it anyway." After saying his prayers, he opened his eyes and his eyes went straight to his daddy's newspaper on the chair. He observed a lifted page and when he opened it, the car key fell off from inside the newspaper and he was happy and grateful to God.

Later on, he told his parents the story of how praying to God had helped him find his daddy's car key.

Things to do: "Prayer is the most important part of your relationship with God."

Activity: Practice five finger prayer:

Thumb – Praise and thank God for His blessings.
Pointer – Ask God to bless your parents and siblings.
Middle – Say a prayer for yourself.
Ring – Say a prayer for your teachers, friends and neighbors.
Little – Say a prayer for the sick, the poor and those in need of your prayers.

Questions:

1. Does God enjoy hearing you speak to Him?
2. Why would God say no to some of your desires?
3. Who are the people that God also wants to bless with you?
4. What should you do when you get into trouble?
5. What are the things you should pray about?

WHAT DID YOU LEARN FROM THIS LESSON?

LESSON ELEVEN

Obedience /əˈbiːdiəns/

Meaning: Listening and doing what someone asks you to do.

Bible text: Children, obey your parents in the Lord, for this is right – Ephesians Chapter 6:1.

Thought: Why should I be asked to do what I don't feel like doing?

To obey can be very difficult especially when it is really against what you want and this is why God has promised blessings to all those who are obedient to Him and to their parents. In the bible, Jonah did not obey God and God caused a big fish to swallow him. Adam and Eve disobeyed God and lost the wonderful things that God prepared for them. But Abraham obeyed God and God made him the father of many nations. Jesus also obeyed God and God became proud of him and gave him a great name. There are many rules that you must obey which includes—do not steal, do not tell lies, do not become proud, and do not hate others or treat them badly.

You should not just obey God but must also obey your parents because they are older and know better than you. They love you and want the best for you and so many times they make a lot of sacrifices for you in order to make you better and happier. To obey them therefore, can be a way of saying thank you to them. So you must take permission from your parents before doing things, listen to them and carry out their instructions. You should also obey your teachers, your school and the government rules.

God has attached the commandment of obedience with a blessing and so when you obey God, your parents, your teachers, and those who care for you, you'll attract God's love, favors and blessings: You will have long life, good health, riches and all will be well with you.

Story: Tony Learnt His Lesson

Tony was a stubborn and disobedient child and his parents were very worried about this. One day, his daddy bought him a bicycle as a gift of love but pleaded with Peter to be obedient to them. He warned Tony to ride the bicycle only within the street and should never ride on the major road. But Tony did not obey. Many times when his parents were not around, he would ride on the major road. One day, as he was riding in excitement, he got distracted. A car passed really near and almost ran over him; he fell to the ground, sprained his ankle and broke his bicycle. Tony could not get up; he lay on the floor and cried bitterly. He regretted to have disobeyed his parents and also wondered what his parents would do when they come back home.

Quote: "Disobedience leads to a downfall."

Things to do: Obey your parents for a week and experience how happy they can be and how much love they can give to you.

Questions:

1. Why is obedience often difficult?
2. Mention some of those who disobeyed God in the bible?
3. Apart from God, who are the other people you should obey?
4. Why should you obey your parents?
5. What are the things you can gain from being obedient?

WHAT DID YOU LEARN FROM THIS LESSON?

LESSON TWELVE

Positive Self-Talk /pɑzətɪv//self/ /tɔːk/

Meaning: Speaking only good things about yourself.

Bible text: I can do all things through Christ who strengthens me – Philippians Chapter 4:13.

Thought: But what if I'm not that good?

The bible says, "Let the weak say I'm strong" and so when you speak positively, it doesn't mean that you lie, it simply means that you want to use your words to claim good things into your life. God created the entire world by His words; He said, "Let there be light and there was light." He has also given us, who are His children, the power to use our words to attract good things into our lives.

There is power in your words. The things you say will eventually come to pass in your life, so why not say only the things that are good and positive. But first, you have to allow your mind to think only good and positive things then you should speak them out and you'll start experiencing them. Believe that you are special because you truly are. Believe that no subject is difficult for you to understand, no work is too hard and no good manner is impossible to learn. Say "I can make it", "I'm good enough", "It will be well with me", "I'm bright and intelligent", "I can be what I want to be", "I will keep trying", "I'm making progress", "I'll not give up" and so on. Don't say things like, "It won't work", "It's impossible", "Nothing will ever go right", "I won't do well with or at something". When you believe good things about yourself and speak them out then you'll have good things come your way and you'll have a great and successful life.

Story: Alice was a girl who believed that she could be anything she wanted to be. She often told her parents, friends, teachers and everyone that she would take her studies seriously and will become a very successful woman when she grows up. Whenever she experienced any difficult situation, she would whisper to herself that she will overcome and she often did. Alice's strong will and desire to be successful made her to excel in all her school subjects and she always came out excellent. Her positive self-talk gave her confidence and made everything easy for her and when she grew up, she started a very big school where she taught children how to use positive self-talk to achieve every good thing that they want from life. Later on, she married a very handsome prince and they lived happily ever after.

Quote: "I tell you the truth, if anyone says to this mountain, "Go, throw yourself into the sea" and does not doubt in his heart but believes that what he says will happen, it will be done for him." – Jesus Christ.

Things to do: Write out five good things you want for your life and start claiming them with your words.

Questions:

1. What did God use to create the entire world?
2. What can you use to attract good things into your life?
3. What are some of the words you should not speak about yourself?
4. What are some of the words you should speak about yourself?
5. Who said, "I tell you the truth, if anyone says to this mountain, "Go, throw yourself into the sea" and does not doubt in his heart but believes that what he says will happen, it will be done for him."?

WHAT DID YOU LEARN FROM THIS LESSON?

LESSON THIRTEEN

Helpfulness /helpflnəs/

Meaning: To do something for someone that will make life or work easier for them.

Bible test: Carry each other's burdens, and in this way, you will fulfill the law of Christ – Galatians Chapter 6:2.

Thought: If I help them, will they help me back?

There is no help you truly give to someone that you'll not receive in some way. The help you give to someone may not always come back to you from the same person but you'll surely get it back in some way.

Helping people is one of the most important things we must do in order to show love for one another. We live for one another and only those who know and practice this are truly on their way to heaven. God gave us hands not just for our own use but also for helping other people. So, we must do all we can to help others with our helping hands.

We can help your parents to keep the house neat and tidy, help to keep the community clean, help the elderly ones with chores and errands, help people to find their lost items, help friends and neighbors when they are in need, help schoolmates and classmates to learn and understand, help the poor and those in need, donate used toys and clothes to the people who don't have any or enough and help everyone that we can.

The quickest way to receive God's love and blessings is by helping others. Also, when you help people, you will be happy and everyone will be pleased with you.

Story: Mother Theresa

Mother Theresa was a woman who was very kind to those in need. She gave a helping hand to a lot of people, especially the poor. She often said, "By feeding and helping the poor, I am feeding and helping Jesus, for that is what he commanded, to help the poor. When I was hungry, did you feed me? When I was

thirsty, did you give me drink? When I was cold, did you clothe me?"
God rewarded and blessed her greatly and today, everyone thinks of Mother Theresa as one of the greatest women the world has ever known.

Quote: "If you give help, you'll always find help when you are in need."

Things to do: Write out five things you can do for others this week and begin to practice them from today.

Questions:

1. What is one of the most important things you must do in order to show love to people?
2. God gave you hands so that you can also do what?
3. What are some of the helps you can give to people?
4. What is the quickest way to receive God's love and blessings?
5. Who are some of the people you should help?

WHAT DID YOU LEARN FROM THIS LESSON?

WHAT DID YOU LEARN FROM THIS LESSON?

LESSON FOURTEEN

Respect /rıspekt/

Meaning: Not doing the things that others dislike. It is also to act in a way that will be good to yourself and to others.

Bible text: So in everything, do to others what you would have them do to you. For this sums up the law and the prophets –Matthew Chapter 7:12.

Thought: Shouldn't I respect only those who deserve to be respected?

Everyone needs respect and one of the best ways to show people that you love them is to treat them with respect. We must learn to respect one another because where there is no respect, people will fight and hate one another and then, there'll be no love, peace and happiness.

You are to respect your parents, yourself, your teachers, your leaders, your seniors and everyone alike. To respect means to love people, to act nicely to them, to be truthful to them, to be polite and to compliment them. It means not calling others bad names or being rude or abusive, not disobeying your parents and seniors and not laughing or making fun of others. It is also to follow rules and instructions, to take permission from your parents or anyone who takes care of you and to apologize when you do something wrong.

Don't speak bad and harshly to people, don't yell, scream or snap at others. Rather, be gentle, listen without interrupting and speak with a smile. When we all practice respect, we'll have better relationships with ourselves and we all will be happy.

Story: Sam and the Old Woman

Sam was a very disrespectful child. He did not respect his parents, teachers, himself and others. He disobeyed, abused and laughed at people. Even though Sam's parents had continued to teach him how to be respectful, he stubbornly refused to learn.

One day, he saw an old woman who was passing by his street and he made fun of her and laughed at how she walked. But Sam did not know that the woman had some powers. While he was busy imitating, laughing and making fun of the old woman, she angrily cursed him and Sam immediately bent and began walking like an old person. Before she walked away, she told Sam that he would continue to walk like that until he learns how to respect people.

Sam became ashamed of himself as everyone made jest of him for what he brought upon himself. He quickly started learning how to respect, though it was not easy for him from the beginning because he was already very used to being disrespectful.

Gradually, he became a very respectful child. He respected his parents, teachers, neighbors and everyone. He greeted people, did not abuse and so on. Sam eventually won the love of everyone and they all prayed that God should restore him to walk normally again. Then suddenly, he straightened and walked uprightly. After Sam got well again, he was not the only one who learned how to be respectful. The other children in his street and school also learnt some lessons.

Quote: "Respect is reciprocal – When you respect others, they too will respect you."

Things to do: Explain to your parents what respect means and tell them how you will show them and others respect.

Questions:

1. What are the things that disrespect can cause?
2. Who are the people you must respect?
3. What are some of the ways to show respect?
4. What will everyone experience if we all learn to respect one another?
5. What is the meaning of respect is reciprocal?

WHAT DID YOU LEARN FROM THIS LESSON?

LESSON FIFTEEN

Beat Shyness /biːt/ /ʃaɪnəs/

Meaning: To be able to overcome shame and timidity.

Bible text: Arise, shine, for your light has come! And the glory of the Lord is risen upon you—Isaiah Chapter 60:1.

Thought: I often wonder what people will think or say about me.

To focus on what people will think or say about you can cause you to be shy and shyness is one of the biggest enemies of success. It could be true that you've always been a shy person but the good news is that you can beat shyness and live a great life that God has given to you. Shyness has no meaningful, value or advantage. It makes people to be timid. Shyness robs people of opportunities. It prevents people from shining with their qualities and abilities and will make their lives boring. It has too many disadvantages and this is why you must have to beat the shyness in you.

When you try something at first, you may not be perfect at it but constant practice will make you perfect. So, even if you fail while trying to shine, never quit, try again and again until you become perfect. If people speak ill of you or laugh at you, never let that bother you because when you become perfect, you would have been better than them. Scientists experiment many times until they find the best method and result and that is what you should always do. Try and keep trying until you become the best you can be.

When you are bold, you'll be able to freely use the qualities and abilities that God gave to you. If you do not beat shyness, shyness will beat you and keep you down. It will cause you to make plenty of mistakes which will still make people to laugh at you. So, you should never let you mind worry about what people will think or say because this will discourage you. When you are bold, out-going and smart, you'll have more fun, make more friends, enjoy school activities more, shine with your gifts and talents, be more useful to your society and then, make your parents and teachers proud.

Story: Thomas Edison

A man named Thomas Edison tried to invent the light bulb. He knew what he wanted to do but he wasn't sure of how to get it done. He tried, tried and tried and failed so many times. People may have laughed at him for trying to do what he could not do but he was not shy and did not let them discourage him. Instead, he continued trying until he eventually invented the light bulb and today, nobody has forgotten that it was Thomas Edison that helped us to have light bulbs in our houses.

Things to do: "Be confident because you are special in your own way."

Activity: Always think of yourself as a super hero who is bold and not shy to say or do wonderful things.

Questions:

1. What can cause you to be shy?
2. What is the advantage of shyness?
3. What does shyness rob from people?
4. What are the bad things that shyness can cause?
5. What are the things that boldness can do for you?

WHAT DID YOU LEARN FROM THIS LESSON?

LESSON SIXTEEN

Study /stʌdi/

Meaning: To spend some time learning something in order to understand and know it fully.

Bible text: Study to show yourself approved unto God (KJV)—2 Timothy Chapter 2:15.

Thought: I wish my books are as interesting as cartoons.

To study may not be very interesting like watching movies, playing or telling stories but it is one of the most important things to do in order to become great in the future. It is good to watch your TV programmes, to play and to have fun but it is better to find time to study. There are so many things to learn in life but the most important thing to learn about is your dream. When you know what you want to become in future, then you have to start learning everything that will make you become great in that thing you want to become. Do you want to become a doctor? Then study everything that will help you become a successful doctor. Do you want to become a fashion designer? Then start studying the things that will help you to become a great fashion designer.

Knowledge will brighten your future and will light up your world. Education is truly the key to a great life. It brings you to the knowledge of your gifts and talents that is, your qualities and abilities, and it helps you to be a confident person.

God hates ignorance because ignorance is a killer and a destroyer. He wants His children to acquire knowledge as much as we can and so He tells us in the bible, "My people perish for lack of knowledge." Ignorance causes a lot of bad things like poverty and shame. When you study, you'll become knowledgeable and will defeat a lot of bad things like ignorance, poverty and shame. You should read your books and your bible. Listen to your teachers and to those who know better than you and when you do not understand, ask questions.

Story: Napoleon Hill

Napoleon Hill was born in a family that was surrounded by poverty and illiteracy. But his step-mother did not accept poverty and ignorance and so she encouraged him to desire knowledge. He started studying about the lives of people who became great by doing great things. He encountered great struggle, hardships, poverty and failure but it was the knowledge he obtained from studying that made him find happiness in abundance and prosperity that was enough for his needs. And he wrote a book that he titled "Think and Grow rich" which teaches people how to be successful by studying to acquire knowledge.

Quote: "Study is for the mind what eating is for the body."

Things to do: Create a particular time for your study and tell your mummy or daddy to always remind you of your study time.

Questions:

1. To be great in the future, what is one of the most important things you must do?
2. What must you learn about?
3. Education is the key to what?
4. What are the bad things that ignorance can cause?
5. How can you overcome ignorance?

WHAT DID YOU LEARN FROM THIS LESSON?

LESSON SEVENTEEN

Honesty /ɑnəsti/

Meaning: To speak the truth and to act truthfully.

Bible text: These are the things you are to do; speak the truth to each other—Zachariah Chapter 8:16a.

Thought: But telling lies often gets me out of trouble.

In the bible, we learn that truthful lips endure forever, but a lying tongue lasts only a moment. This means that when you tell the truth, it sets you free permanently but lies can get you out of trouble only for a moment and then will get you into a bigger trouble when the truth is discovered. Lies don't save and if you feel that truth can't save you, then you should better know that lies will destroy you. Lies causes confusion, troubles and a lot of bad things.

You can forget the lies you told and then speak more lies but truth once spoken remains the same. God's words are true and He hates lies. He commands us to always speak the truth because only the truth can set us free. And if you ever get into any trouble for telling the truth, then God will take the responsibility to deliver you. Being honest is not just about speaking the truth, it also means to act in the right way. When you speak and act in a right way then you are honest.

Don't tell lies or make up rumors, say exactly how something happened. Don't deceive, cheat, steal or do bad things but if you do, don't hide them. Accept your actions even if you'll get into trouble. It pays to be honest. When you are honest, you'll have a free conscience, you'll enjoy the love and blessings of God and you'll also have inner peace.

Story: Ola and the Math Test

Ola was a very smart and clever boy. He often got good remarks from his teachers who were very proud of him. But Ola became very proud with himself that he did not study anymore. The mathematics teacher had announced that there was going to be a mathematics test but Ola did not study. He was too confident in his ability to pass that he had decided not to study for the test.

The test was set and they were asked to begin. He looked at the question again and again and it became obvious to him that he didn't know how to solve it to get to the answer. He looked sideways and saw his classmates who were not even his match solving the math confidently and he imagined the shame he'll face if he submits an empty sheet. He was still thinking of what to do when he heard the teacher announce that they should round off. Ola was shocked and he panicked. He quickly decided to cheat rather than face the shame of submitting an empty sheet.

Jack, the dumbest student in the class had intentionally sat close to Ola in order to copy from him but when he realized that Ola was not writing, he started to solve the mathematics in his own way to avoid submitting an empty sheet. But Ola in fear forgot that Jack was a dumb student. He rolled his eyes to the right into Jack's sheet and copied everything Jack wrote as quickly as he could. After the test, he walked away, feeling better that he, at least, wrote something.

The next day, the teacher came to the class with their sheets. With an angry look on his face he called up Jack and Ola. Both of them had scored zero. He asked them to speak the truth about who copied from each other. While Jack pointed at Ola, Ola pointed at Jack. Curious about the truth, he wrote down the question on two different sides of the board and asked them to solve the question in front of everyone. As usual, Jack got busy solving nonsense but Ola did not know the math and stood like a tree in front of everyone. It was a big shame for him as everyone laughed and wondered at what had happened to him. After that incident, Ola decided that he must always study and must never cheat or be dishonest again.

Quote: "Honesty is the first chapter in the book of wisdom." – Thomas Jefferson.

Things to do: Have you decided to tell only the truth? If yes, then tell your parents about it and also tell them not to buy you any present if you tell a lie.

Questions:

1. Can lies get you out of trouble permanently?
2. What can set you free?
3. What else does honesty mean apart from speaking the truth?
4. What are the ways you can be dishonest?
5. What are the good things you can get from being honest?

WHAT DID YOU LEARN FROM THIS LESSON?

LESSON EIGHTEEN

Punctuality /pʌŋktʃuæləti/

Meaning: To do something or to arrive somewhere early, at the right time or at the time you are not late.

Bible text: There is a time for everything and a season for every activity under heaven—Ecclesiastes Chapter 3:1.

Thought: Do I really have to be there before an activity begins?

Time works on its own and it's nobody's friend. It ticks gently but can pass very fast. It waits for no one and so, you must learn to work with it and do things at their appropriate times. You have to respect time because time is precious. Time lost can never be recovered. Everything has its time therefore, you must learn to give everything their full time.

You know you have to get your homework done but you say to yourself "Later, after my favorite TV show." If you choose to take the maybe, later approach, that could make somethings go wrong. So, don't make putting off things a habit and don't be too slow in doing things. Tardiness, laziness and procrastination are big causes of lateness. Time can pass very fast and so you must begin on time as to make it on time because it's best to be at an event before it begins.

There are many bad things that lateness can cause. It can cause noise, distraction and rowdiness at the event. It can make others to be unhappy with you for making them wait for you and waste their own time. It shows that you don't care, it can make other activities go wrong and then, it can cause you to panic, rush and have stress.

But to be punctual helps you not to be hasty and to panic, it helps you to get a good seat and also to be fully ready before the event begins. It makes you not to miss out anything, it also shows that you respect time, care for others and are interested in the event. When you are on time, you can also help to set up the venue for the event for example, your classroom or your church and this kind of good behavior will make people appreciate you, respect you, trust and depend on you and then learn from you.

Story: God's Reward for Punctuality

A particular church had a large congregation and God loved to be present in the church but he had a problem with the members because too many of them were always late for church activities. Most of them gave various reasons for their lateness. Some would say, "They woke up late, they looked for their clothes, shoes or watches." Others would say, "Time went very fast, they needed to finish up with somethings or it was too rainy or sunny." Most times, God would come and wait for too long before a lot of them would stroll in and He was just not pleased with this because He wanted to have His full worship time. And so, He planned to do something. He started taking note of the early comers and observed that they were just the same people and He was pleased with them.

One Sunday morning, He poured down the rain heavily and arrived at the church quite early. He came along with lots and lots of blessings and wrote a "Thank you for your punctuality" note on each of the blessings. Despite the rain, the early comers came early as usual. And when they came, they met these blessings all over the church and were so very happy and grateful to God. They had too many blessings that their hands could not carry. They had to go home about three to four times to drop some of their many blessings. While this was happening, some people were still observing the rain and relaxing in their houses. But the news about the blessings travelled so fast and got to the ears of the late comers who didn't mind the rain anymore and ran as fast as they could to the church only to find out that it was too late for them because God had gone back to heaven with the remaining blessings. They were all disappointed at themselves and regretted why they were not punctual.

Quote: "Show some mercy to your time, don't always waste it." – Amit Kalantri.

Things to do: Plan your time to help you keep to time by writing down things like:

Brush my mouth - 3 Minutes.
Take a bathe – 5 Minutes.
Get dressed – 12 Minutes.

Eat breakfast – 15 Minutes.

Get to school – 10 Minutes.

Get a timer and note down how long each activity actually takes, then master the timing.

Questions:

1. Is time anyone's friend?
2. Why should you respect time?
3. What are the bad things that lateness can cause?
4. What can you achieve by being punctual?
5. What are some of the things that can cause you to be late for an activity?

WHAT DID YOU LEARN FROM THIS LESSON?

LESSON NINTEEN

Tolerance /tɑlərəns/

Meaning: To take it easy with people and to accept them for who they are.

Bible text: Be completely humble and gentle; be patient, bearing with one another in love - Ephesians Chapter 4:2.

Thought: Why can't people do things the usual way?

Life does not have a particular "usual way" because things were meant to be different. God created us to be different and so we are all different. We act differently, see things differently, understand things differently and also want and enjoy different things but God did not create a different world for each of us. He created only one world for us all and commands us to love and accept one another. As people live, work and do things together, they will hurt each other. Sometimes, you'll hurt people and people will hurt you. But to tolerate is to understand that people are different and to accept them as they are. You have to accept people's gender, race and social status.

You have to learn to tolerate people because some people will have to tolerate you. People who are not perfect are imperfect and we are all imperfect, only God is perfect and as God tolerates our imperfections likewise we should learn to tolerate others imperfections.

You have to also know that being tolerant does not mean to accept bad behavior such as disrespect, bullying or stealing. These kinds of behavior should not be accepted, they should rather be reported.

When someone does not choose your way, makes a mistake or offends you that is when you should show tolerance for this is a way to love.

Story: Ruth Could Not Be Changed

Mary, Elizabeth and Ruth were three sisters who really liked to spend time together. Mary and Elizabeth loved to watch cartoons while Ruth always loved to play rhymes. Mary and Elizabeth wanted to change Ruth to make her stop playing and enjoying rhymes and to start watching cartoons with them.

One day, they planned to hide and then later, dispose Ruth's rhyming CD in order to make her have no other choice but to start watching cartoons with them. They hid the CD where she could not find it. When Ruth did not find her CD, she disturbed the whole house; searched and searched and cried and cried so loudly that her sisters did not even enjoy their cartoon anymore. They endured, thinking Ruth would stop disturbing after a day or two but that did not happen. Ruth refused to eat any food, did not talk to any of them, still continued her search and still cried out loudly.

After two full days, Mary and Elizabeth understood that they could not change Ruth and that trying will only cause the three of them to be unhappy. They finally decided to make themselves happy by confessing to their sister who forgave them and they all learnt to tolerate their differences by taking turns to play their cartoons and rhymes.

Quote: Tolerance is the key to building a lasting relationship.

Things to do: What are some of the things you don't like about your best friend and how do you manage to tolerate these things? Practice tolerating others as you tolerate your best friend.

Questions:

1. We are all different but God created only one world for us and commands us to do what?
2. We are all imperfect; therefore we should do what to one another?
3. What are some of the behaviors that should be reported and not tolerated?
4. When should you tolerate people?
5. What are some of the ways you can tolerate people?

WHAT DID YOU LEARN FROM THIS LESSON?

LESSON TWENTY

Gratitude /ɡrætɪtud/

Meaning: To be thankful for what someone has done for you or has given you.

Bible text: In everything give thanks, for this is the will of God in Christ Jesus for you - I Thessalonians Chapter 5:18.

Thought: But I could forget to say thank you.

It is not always very easy to do something good to people and so when someone does something good to you, you should never forget to say thank you. It is wrong to forget to be thankful. If you do not learn to say thank you, everyone will know you as an ungrateful person and no one likes to relate with an ungrateful person.

God has created the world for us and has provided in it everything that we need to have a great life and for this, we must be grateful. God also specially created you in His image and likeness and made no one else like you. He gave you special gifts and talents and has promised to always be with you. You should therefore, be grateful for God's love and should always begin your prayers with "thank you God" and also end with "I thank you God for listening to my prayers."

You should be grateful for your parents love and care, for your gifts and talents, for days and nights, for sun and rain, for air and water, for plants and food and for friends and loved ones. When you count your blessings and name them one by one, you'll have many things you'll be grateful for.

Those who are grateful are the happiest people on earth but if you are often sad and grumpy, then, it is because you have not been grateful. You should let your parents know you love them by being grateful to them. Say thank you to those who help you or do things for you and to those who teach or correct you. Say thank you or I'm grateful.

Thankfulness is very important because it attracts a lot of blessings into our lives but unthankfulness prevents us from receiving blessings and only wicked and cruel people don't say thank you.

Story: Jesus and the Lepers

Ten men were sick. They were lepers. They desperately wanted to be healed and so they came to meet Jesus and begged Him for mercy. Jesus was moved to help them and so he instructed them on what to do. As they were going to show themselves to the priest as Jesus had instructed them, they all got cleansed but nine of them forgot to come to Jesus to say thank you. Only one of them went back to Jesus and said a big thank you to Him. This pleased Jesus and He blessed the man and made him totally well.

Quote: Being grateful with a smile and cheerfulness is the best way to say thank you.

Things to do: In your special gratitude notebook or journal, put down some things that you are grateful for each day and thank God for them.

Questions:

1. Should you ever forget to say thank you? Why?
2. How is the best way to say thank you?
3. How should you begin your prayers?
4. What are some of the things you should be grateful for?
5. What kinds of people don't say thank you?

WHAT DID YOU LEARN FROM THIS LESSON?

Meaning of hard words:

1. Accidentally: When something happen by accident.
2. Admired: To look at someone or something with joy or pleasure.
3. Apologize: To say you are sorry to someone for hurting them or causing them trouble.
4. Attractive: To be pretty and to be pleasant to look at.
5. Bacteria: An organism that can cause disease.
6. Bullied: To use force, power or threat to frighten someone else.
7. Champion: To be a winner in something.
8. Cheered: To be happy and excited.
9. Confess: To accept that you did something.
10. Congregation: The people who attend a church service.
11. Curious: To want to know more about something.
12. Desperately: To need or want something very much indeed.
13. Determine: The reason or cause of something.
14. Discovered: To find out or learn about something.
15. Dwelt: To live at a place.
16. Encouragement: To give someone hope or confidence.
17. Excited: To be very happy about something in a way that you cannot relax
18. Grip: To hold something strongly or firmly.
19. Grumpy: To be unhappy, sad or miserable.
20. Imagination: To think about pictures or things that are not real.
21. Infection: A disease that is caused by germs or bacteria.
22. Interaction: To have a talk with someone.
23. Invent: To think and make out something.
24. Laziness: To avoid work or to be too slow to do something.
25. Littered: To scatter rubbish around.
26. Justice: To punish someone for an offence.
27. Maturity: To be fully developed in your behavior.
28. Negative: To think of the bad things of something instead of the good things.
29. Neighborhood: A place or a town where people live.
30. Observed: To notice something.
31. Opportunity: The time or situation that is right to do something.
32. Orderliness: To be well-organized and controlled.

33. Positive: To think of the good aspect of a situation instead of bad ones.
34. Procrastination: To leave the things that you should do until later.
35. Relationship: The way people behave and feel towards each other.
36. Regardless: To not let something to affect another thing.
37. Regret: To wish that something did not happen.
38. Relaxed: To be calm and not worried.
39. Responsibility: To have a job or a duty.
40. Rowdiness: To be noisy or rough.
41. Rudeness: To speak or act in a way that offends others.
42. Sacrifice: To give up something for someone or for something else.
43. Scared: To frighten someone or something to go away.
44. Talent: Your ability to do something well.
45. Tardiness: To be slow to act.
46. Task: The work that you have to do.
47. Timid: To be shy and to have no courage or confidence.
48. Treasure: The thing that you think is special to you.
49. Wail: To make a long and loud cry.
50. Wrinkle: The lines or folds that forms on people's faces when they frown or grow old.

About the author

Chinonye Oluoha is an educator, motivational speaker, and author. With her degree in education and a full commitment to God the Father, she expertly teaches and motivates people about how to attain the greatness that God has destined for them. She enjoys teaching and writing for God's glory.

Other books by Chinonye Oluoha: *Basic Life Principles for Raising Virtuous Children, tweens and teens Volumes 1 and 2, Awaken your greatness, Raising future leaders and poetry on morals and virtues.*

Contact:
Phone: +2349094949467.
Blog: Www.wellofwaters.com
Emails: Wellofwaters@gmail.com.